OUR BABY

OUR BABY

Tony Bradman & Lynn Breeze

Collins
An Imprint of HarperCollinsPublishers

Our baby can't get out of bed...

but I can.

Our baby can't use the potty...

but I can.

Our baby can't wash herself...

but I can.

Our baby can't do up her clothes...

but I can.

Our baby can't get down from the table...

but I can.

Our baby can't climb the stairs...

but I can.

Our baby can't go everywhere...

but I can.

Our baby can't play with my toys...

but I can.

And sometimes, Mum and Dad can't...

stop our baby crying.

But I can.

First published in Great Britain by HarperCollins Publishers Ltd in 1995
ISBN 0 00 761366 0   Text copyright © Tony Bradman 1995. Illustrations copyright © Lynn Breeze 1995
HarperCollins Publishers Ltd, 77-85 Fulham Palace Road, Hammersmith, London W6 8JB. Printed and bound in Singapore